British
and American
Flintlocks

Frederick Wilkinson

COUNTRY LIFE COLLECTORS' GUIDES

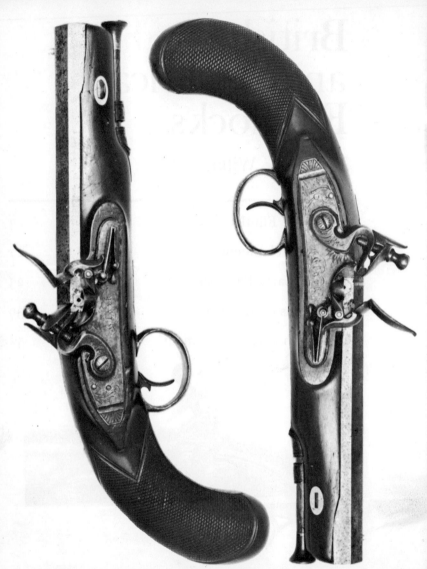

Pair of pistols made about 1810 by Clark of London, with octagonal barrels and platinum lined touch-holes. The butts are cross-hatched with a plain base. Overall length 11·25 in. Length of barrel 6·12 in. Calibre ·62 in. Durrant Collection.

Before the Flintlock

Numbers in the margin refer to the page where an illustration may be found

Of prime importance to the soldier or hunter is the reliability of his firearm, for without this all the skill and care that have gone into the production of the weapon, and all the time and trouble spent in training and practice are wasted. Reliability, as far as antique firearms were concerned, was always somewhat uncertain and even with the highest quality weapons there was an ever present element of doubt as to whether the weapon would fire. Probably the simplest and surest method of ensuring ignition of the gunpowder was to ignite it directly with a flame and this obvious system was used for the earliest firearms. Gunpowder had originated far away in ancient China and its secret had moved slowly, carried by Arab travellers, explorers and armies, only reaching Europe in a practical and useable form early in the 14th century. It was a simple mixture of sulphur, charcoal and saltpetre but in its early days composition was uncertain and performance erratic. Despite all these disadvantages gunpowder did present a very serious threat to the erstwhile supreme ruler of the battlefield – the armoured knight. It gave to even the simplest soldier the ability to strike down the most completely armoured man on the field.

Technique was simple and could be mastered by almost anyone with a few minutes instruction. Powder and wad were poured down the barrel and a ball of lead, stone or iron was rammed home on top of the charge, the weapon then being ready. To fire it a glowing piece of coal, smouldering tow or even a hot iron was touched to the powder by way of a small hole, thus setting off a chemical reaction which produced an explosion. By the beginning of the 15th century the firing process had been somewhat mechanised by the introduction of an ingenious double-curved arm, the serpentine. In one end was fixed a length of cord which had been impregnated with a mixture of saltpetre in varying strengths so that when it dried it would burn with a slow, spluttering, glowing end. Pressure on the lower arm of the serpentine caused the upper arm to move forward and down so placing the glowing end of the match into a pan mounted at the side of the touch-hole and holding a small amount of gunpowder known as the priming. As this priming flashed the spark ignited the main charge and so fired the weapon.

4   The so-called **matchlock system** was basic, simple and reliable but it did suffer from a number of very serious drawbacks. The difficulty of maintaining a glowing end to the match was considerable since wind and rain or accidents could so easily extinguish the glowing spark and leave the musketeer defenceless, at the mercy of his enemy. There were also serious practical problems in the mere handling of the glowing match with loose powder about. The sum effect of all these problems was to limit

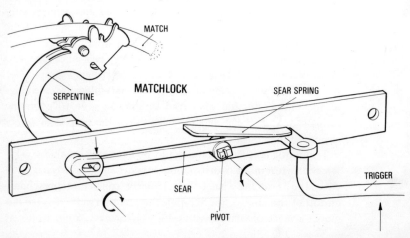

MATCH

MATCHLOCK

SERPENTINE

SEAR SPRING

SEAR

PIVOT

TRIGGER

the use of matchlocks to infantry but these long, cumbersome and heavy muskets, weighing many pounds and over five or six feet long, were issued to the armies of most European monarchs. It was the matchlock that the early settlers took to America and these weapons are variously described in the documents of the time as arquebusses, calivers and muskets. The exact meaning is not always clear but essentially the difference was that the term arquebus was applied to any form of firearm whilst the musket was the long shoulder arm and the caliver was a slightly smaller version. If the European found the matchlock cumbersome and awkward to use, how much more so must the settlers of early America have found it. In most battles of the period the musketeers were in set ranks and positions and movement was fairly limited so that the hindrance of the musket was not too important, but the colonist of the New World was faced with a quick, savage enemy excelling in ambush and sudden attack. The glowing match immediately betrayed the colonist's position to his enemy; a sudden downpour of rain and he was defenceless. There were constant dangers of accidental explosion and even when functioning properly accuracy was probably less than that of the Indian's bow. However, they were the only firearms

Detail of wheellock on a pistol of about 1620. The wheel cover and studs are gilt. Overall length of pistol 19 in. Bennett Collection.

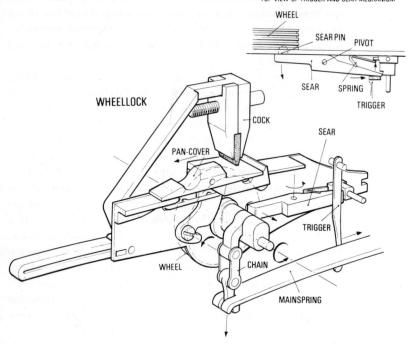

WHEEL

SEAR PIN

PIVOT

SEAR

SPRING

TRIGGER

WHEELLOCK

COCK

SEAR

PAN-COVER

TRIGGER

WHEEL

CHAIN

MAINSPRING

readily available and no doubt the colonists valued them highly.

There was another type of ignition available, known as the
wheellock. Although it did overcome a number of the inherent
difficulties of the matchlock system it was a rather complex and
delicate mechanism. The glowing match was replaced by a
mechanical system for producing sparks. A piece of pyrites, a
readily available mineral, was held between two jaws and pressed
firmly against the roughened edge of a rotating steel wheel. To
prepare the mechanism for firing, the wheel was rotated by means
of a key or spanner; this compressed a strong V spring and the
wheel was then locked in this position. Pressure on the trigger
withdrew the locking bar and the torque exerted by the spring
caused the wheel to rotate rapidly. Friction between the edge of
the wheel and the· pyrites produced a stream of sparks which

5, 6

ignited the priming-powder to fire the main charge. This system represented a considerable technological improvement for the user could now do something impossible with the matchlock, in that the wheellock weapon could be loaded, primed, spanned and then placed on one side ready for instant use without requiring any further attention. There was now no inherent danger from the naked glowing tip of the match. Wheellocks could also be carried safely, since the arm holding the pyrites could be pivoted clear of the wheel so that even if the trigger were pressed and the wheel rotated there would be no sparks and no shot. No longer was the soldier betrayed by the glowing match in the dark and he was now far less at the mercy of the weather. With all these great advantages it might have been expected that the new system would have been universally adopted but, as with all things, it was not without its limitations. The skill required in manufacture was considerable; repairs were very complicated compared with those required by the matchlock and the action was not always reliable, having a tendency to jam, but probably the greatest limiting factor was the expense. To construct the rather complex gears, levers, chains and wheels required time and skill, particularly with the tools then available; this meant that the finished lock was expensive, and this in turn ensured that its issue would be limited, for few could afford it.

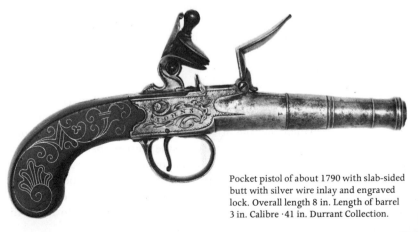

Pocket pistol of about 1790 with slab-sided butt with silver wire inlay and engraved lock. Overall length 8 in. Length of barrel 3 in. Calibre ·41 in. Durrant Collection.

In England wheellocks were mostly imported from Italy and Germany, and the same circumstances would have applied to the American colonies, but evidence of the use of the wheellock by the early settlers in America is somewhat limited. Some were certainly used although it is often argued that the limited financial resources of the early settlers would have precluded the purchase of such expensive items. This may well have been the case in general but undoubtedly rich merchants, government officials and the like possessed these desirable weapons, in which case those that were in use in the New World would certainly have been of the type common in Britain and Europe.

Early examples of wheellocks were normally of rather elaborate form with sundry safety devices and catches on the lockplate, whilst German makers favoured pistols with very large ball butts, frequently covered overall with inlay, and such weapons feature in many English portraits of the period. As the 16th century progressed construction tended to become less complex while decoration became an outstanding feature of this type of weapon, whether pistol or long hunting rifle. Many were beautifully decorated with inlay of precious metals, pewter, mother-of-pearl or, indeed, any decorative material, for all were used to embellish these highly attractive weapons.

The introduction of the wheellock not only revolutionised the ignition systems but also made possible for the first time the construction of small, portable, personal weapons, for owing to the mechanical difficulties involved in their construction and use small matchlock weapons seem to have been extremely rare in Europe, although examples of Japanese matchlock pistols are far more common. Wheellocks of any size could be made without undue trouble and fitted to a weapon no more than a few inches in length, and to these was given the name pistol. A number of explanations for the origin of the term exist but none is conclusive. However, it seems that the most probable explanation is that the term originated in the town of Pistoia in Italy, which was well known for its arms construction during the 16th century. In England these small weapons were usually described as dags and this term continued in use until well into the 17th century, although the term pistol began to gain current usage from about 1570.

The wheellock represented a great step forward in firearms design but its expense and technical complexity precluded its general adoption, and it was not until the appearance of the flintlock system of ignition that firearms, both pistols and long arms, became in any sense commonplace. It was to the domestic system of fire-making that the designers turned for inspiration and at some time during the first half of the 16th century a far simpler device known as the **snaphaunce** was developed. Its design was based on the idea of striking sparks between steel and flint or pyrites, though pyrites was fairly soon abandoned in favour of the more readily available flint. Loading was essentially the same as for all earlier firearms in that a charge of powder was poured down the barrel into the breech and a wad inserted to keep it in place. A ball was then pushed down the barrel by means of the long thin ramrod until it sat securely on top of the wad. A small hole, known as the touch-hole, pierced the side

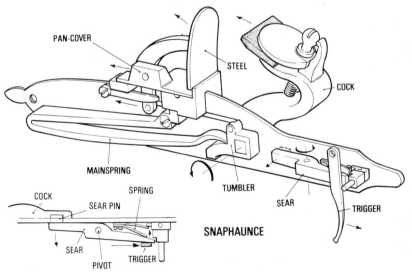

PAN-COVER

STEEL

COCK

MAINSPRING

TUMBLER

SEAR

TRIGGER

SNAPHAUNCE

COCK

SEAR PIN

SPRING

SEAR

PIVOT

TRIGGER

TOP VIEW OF TRIGGER AND SEAR MECHANISM

of the barrel at the breech, where there was a small plate-like projection with a saucer shaped depression; into this depression was deposited a small amount of fine gunpowder known as the priming. When the sparks were struck between flint and steel they fell on to the priming-powder, which ignited, and the flash passed through the touch-hole to the main charge and so fired the projectile.

The first experiments in this direction appear to have been made in the 1540s for there are references in Italian and Swedish manuscripts which would seem, without any real doubt, to refer to a form of lock which utilised the principle of flint striking on steel. The earliest surviving example of the lock occurs on a Swedish weapon which dates from 1556. This comprises a flat lockplate to the outside of which is fitted a long V spring whose tip presses against the toe or forward projection at the base of the cock, a short arm of metal with two long jaws. A piece of flint was placed between the two jaws and a screw tightened to hold it firmly in position. As the cock was drawn back a small spring-operated arm, the sear, projected through the lockplate and engaged with a projection at the rear of the cock, the heel. The cock was now firmly locked in the rear position and would remain so until the sear was withdrawn. Situated above the pan was a sliding pan-cover which could be opened or closed manually, a feature which was common to both the snaphaunce and the matchlock. Also mounted on the outside of the lockplate was an angled arm to the end of which was fitted a flat steel plate. To fire the snaphaunce the barrel was charged in the normal fashion and a pinch of priming-powder placed in the pan which was then covered by the pivoted pan-cover. The steel arm was swung down so that it rested just above the pan and the mechanism was prepared for firing by pulling back the cock until the toe was locked into position by the spring-operated sear. The priming-pan cover was then swung clear and if the trigger were now pressed the sear was withdrawn, allowing the mainspring to push the cock forward so that the flint, gripped firmly by the jaws, struck against the flat surface of the steel and the sparks so produced fell into the priming-powder. At

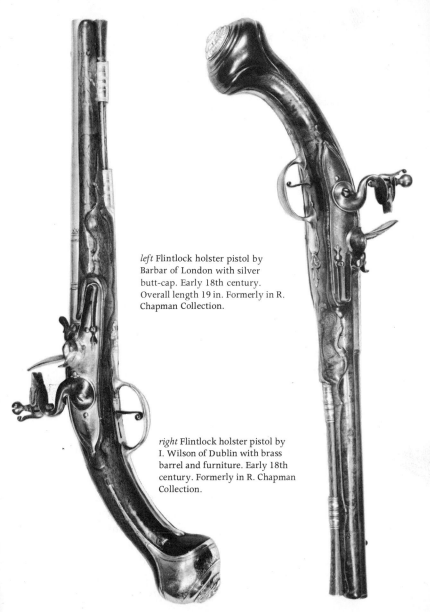

left Flintlock holster pistol by
Barbar of London with silver
butt-cap. Early 18th century.
Overall length 19 in. Formerly in R.
Chapman Collection.

right Flintlock holster pistol by
I. Wilson of Dublin with brass
barrel and furniture. Early 18th
century. Formerly in R. Chapman
Collection.

11

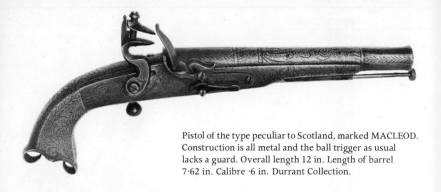

Pistol of the type peculiar to Scotland, marked MACLEOD. Construction is all metal and the ball trigger as usual lacks a guard. Overall length 12 in. Length of barrel 7·62 in. Calibre ·6 in. Durrant Collection.

the same instant of time the steel was pushed clear by the impetus of the cock. There were no safety devices fitted on these early examples such as had been common on the wheellock but the mechanism could, of course, be rendered safe simply by pushing the steel clear of the firing position. This basic lock was commonly used in the northern parts of Europe and as such has been designated the Baltic lock but it was not, in fact, limited to this particular area alone.

This then was the basic snaphaunce mechanism, which was to continue in use for only a comparatively limited period as simpler methods were being developed. Baltic locks seem to have been the earliest form and no doubt the design spread over much of Europe, it being quite conceivable that one or two of them found their way to the American colonies. However, improvements were soon to appear for as early as 1570 German gunsmiths had produced a mechanism which was housed mainly inside the wooden stock, and although this involved cutting away the stock to accommodate the mechanism it did make for a more compact and better protected lock. The shape of the cock evolved from the rather long, slightly curved serpentine appearance of the Baltic lock to a more upright type with double jaws fitted at the top. This squat cock was also fitted to an internal tumbler, a shaped metal bar, and it was on this that the mainspring now pressed rather than directly on the toe of the cock. Further sophistication was introduced in the form of an automatically opening pan-cover, for obviously there was a constant danger that a lapse of memory on the part of the user might mean leaving the pan covered so that the sparks would fail to ignite the priming and a misfire would result. A simple internal connection between the cock and pan-cover on these improved mechanisms ensured that as the cock swung forward the pan-cover was automatically pushed clear, leaving the way open for the sparks to fall into the priming and so ignite the main charge.

It seems likely that this form of mechanism, with the sear operating through the lockplate, reached England around 1570–1580. It would therefore seem highly probable that the first

Fine quality Scottish pistol by Alex Campbell of Doune, a renowned centre of manufacture for these weapons. On the butt and plaque are the motto and crest of the Cameron family. Peter Dale Ltd.

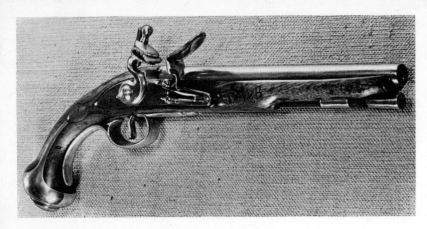

Military pistol, its barrel marked ROYAL HORSE GUARD. Lock marked TOWER and dated 1756. Length of barrel 10 in. Kellam Collection.

examples reached America shortly afterwards. Certainly early colonial records frequently mention the snaphaunce but it is fairly certain that in the majority of cases the weapon referred to is a more conventional flintlock. It is recorded by H.L. Peterson in his *Arms and Armour in Colonial America* that up to the time of writing (1956) only half a dozen fragments of snaphaunces had been discovered at any of the numerous sites of early colonies so far excavated.

Many of these early snaphaunce pistols still closely resembled the wheellock in style and general appearance, with the butt terminating in the ball pommel characteristic of so many wheellock pistols. Lockplates generally speaking were large, and many surviving examples of the late 16th and early 17th centuries are fitted with a ball trigger and lack a trigger-guard, a common feature of most types of firearms of all periods.

Quite soon after the introduction of the basic principles of the snaphaunce a logical step was taken somewhere in Europe in combining the pan-cover and the steel into a single L-shaped piece of metal. The L-shaped piece of steel, known variously as the battery or, to most collectors, as the frizzen, was pivoted

Sea Service pistol of about 1800 with side belt hook but with the unusual feature of a brass barrel inscribed DUBLIN CASTLE. Length of barrel 12 in. Kellam Collection.

Duelling pistol made by Henshall about 1810, with octagonal barrel and ramrod attached by swivel link. Overall length 14 in. Length of barrel 9 in. Calibre ·65 in. Durrant Collection.

at the end of the short arm, which was so placed that in the 'closed' position the shorter arm covered the pan and the long arm stood vertically. The method of operation was now even simpler than that of the snaphaunce. When the trigger was pressed and the cock swung forward the piece of flint rubbed down the face of the upright arm of the frizzen, producing sparks; this very action automatically pushed the frizzen forward so that the pan was uncovered at exactly the same instant, allowing the sparks to drop into the priming and so discharge the weapon. This innovation appeared at a very early date—certainly examples are recorded as early as 1580—however it is not until the beginning of the 17th century that the true flint-lock seems to have appeared on the scene.

Early Developments

18   The true **flintlock** seems to have been originated by a French gunsmith, Marin Le Bourgeois, probably during the second decade of the 17th century. This type of lock did not in fact introduce any completely new features but rather combined several well-established ones into a single, compact, reliable lock. Most of the snaphaunce locks operated with a sear, or small arm, which protruded through the lockplate, but the French lock differed in that the sear was mounted and operated internally. Marin Le Bourgeois utilised a system already known whereby the cock was fitted to a tumbler, a shaped block of metal mounted on the inside of the lockplate and attached to the cock. On the thick edge of the tumbler were cut two notches, and pressing against the edge was the spring-activated sear. As the cock was pulled back the tumbler rotated and the sear slid along the edge until it slipped into the first notch, which was so deep that the movement transmitted by the trigger was insufficient to disengage the sear from the notch, or bent, so that it was virtually impossible to fire the weapon. This safety position is known as the half-cock position and became a common feature of the great majority of flint and percussion weapons. If the cock was now pulled back further the tumbler turned and disengaged the sear from the first bent, allowing it to re-engage with the second and far shallower notch. In this, the full-cock position, the movement afforded by the trigger was sufficient to withdraw the sear and allow the cock, under the pressure

FLINTLOCK

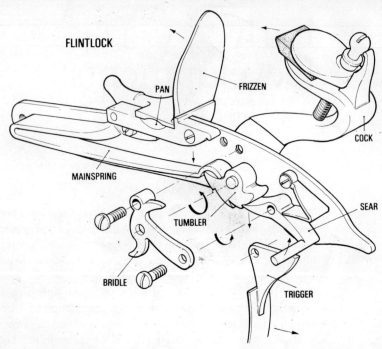

PAN   **FRIZZEN**   **COCK**

MAINSPRING

TUMBLER   **SEAR**

BRIDLE   **TRIGGER**

of the mainspring, to swing forward and strike sparks from
the frizzen. The other feature which Le Bourgeois incorporated
was the one-piece battery. This type of lock is accepted by the
purists as being the only real flintlock in that it satisfies two
requirements set out by the great pioneer of firearms history,
Dr Torsten Lenk, namely that it has a one-piece steel and pan-
cover and a vertically operating sear rather than the lateral one
which protruded through the lockplate of the snaphaunce.
Collectors are generally a little less discriminating as the dis-
tinguishing feature they recognise is simply the combined pan-
cover and steel and they accept as flintlocks some locks which
the purist would assert are not true flintlocks.

This French lock was to form the basic pattern for all flintlock
weapons for the next 130 years but naturally there were variations on this basic theme. The vast majority of British firearms
from the middle of the 17th century used only the French lock.

On the American continent, with its strong Spanish and Portuguese connections, there was, especially in the southern parts, considerable use of the variation known as the Miguelet lock. The basic external features of the Spanish Miguelet lock are easily recognised as the mainspring is mounted on the outside of the lockplate and presses not on to a tumbler as in the case of the French flintlock, but directly upwards on to the rear end, or heel, of the cock. When the cock was pulled back a small, horizontally operating stud projected through the lockplate and engaged with the toe to hold it in the half-cock position. If the cock was then pulled back further the toe was disengaged from the slotted stud and a second, blade-like sear projected through the lockplate and engaged the toe to hold the full-cock position. Pressure on the trigger withdrew both sears and so allowed the cock to fly forward and fire the priming.

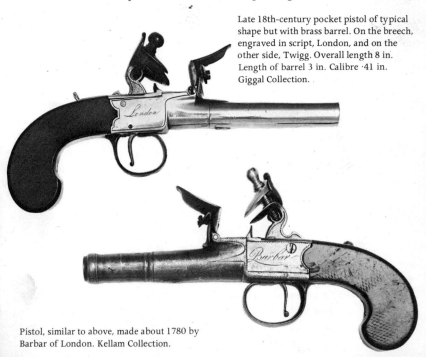

Late 18th-century pocket pistol of typical shape but with brass barrel. On the breech, engraved in script, London, and on the other side, Twigg. Overall length 8 in. Length of barrel 3 in. Calibre ·41 in. Giggal Collection.

Pistol, similar to above, made about 1780 by Barbar of London. Kellam Collection.

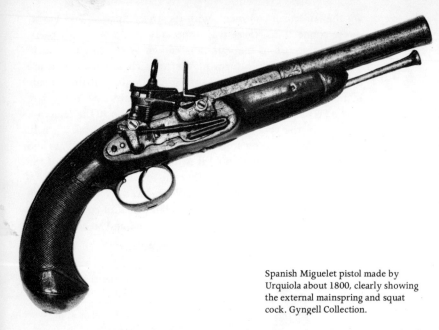

Spanish Miguelet pistol made by Urquiola about 1800, clearly showing the external mainspring and squat cock. Gyngell Collection.

20   Another feature which makes this **Spanish Miguelet lock** easily recognisable is the cock, which was squat with rectangular-shaped jaws. Since the mainspring was usually very powerful it was deemed advisable to afford a means of getting a firm grip, and a ring was fitted to the screw holding the jaws together. Steels were also rather small and the face was frequently, although not invariably, cut with vertical grooves, whilst the small V spring which held the frizzen closed was often covered with a decorative plate.

A variety of the Spanish Miguelet lock was produced in the Madrid area during most of the 18th century and externally this resembled the conventional French lock. Cocks were very similar in shape to the north European swan shape although the screw retained the ring found on conventional Miguelet locks. Madrid locks differed in that the mainspring was mounted internally but the half-cock position was held by means of a stud which protruded through the lockplate and engaged with a small hook-like projection on the lower front section of the cock.

Miguelet locks remained practically unaltered in design throughout the entire period of their use ranging from the early 17th century to well on in the 19th century. Spanish firearms of all types were fitted with Miguelet locks and many must have found their way to the southern areas of North America and

English flintlock pistol with dog catch made by Ralph Venn about 1650. This weapon is broadly typical of pistols of this period with square-ended butt. Overall length 17·25 in. Formerly in R. Chapman Collection.

much of South America. Pistols were often decorated with brass or silver inlay and frequently have a belt hook. This is a bar-like projection fitted to the stock on the side opposite the lock, enabling the pistol to be carried simply by tucking the bar under the belt or sash.

Whilst the Miguelet and Madrid locks may have been more common in the southern areas of America, in the north the more traditional European style would certainly have been far more plentiful. Excavations on the sites of some of the early colonies have revealed remnants of the so-called English lock and the dog lock, both of which represent a sort of intermediate step between the snaphaunce and the French flintlock. The mechanism is somewhat of a mixture in that both these locks have an internal sear, operated in a horizontal plane and engaging with notches or recesses cut into the cock. Both English and dog locks had a **safety device** in the form of a small hook which swung forward to engage with a notch cut in the back of the cock. This device was used to hold the half-cock position and was found on British firearms until the middle of the 17th century. Both types of lock were fitted on pistols and long arms but were gradually abandoned as the French type of lock became predominant.

Although the French lock underwent no major modifications for the whole of its working life there were alterations designed to improve its efficiency. On the early English locks the cock was made with an arm projecting at right angles. The tumbler fitted over this arm and was held in place by a small retaining pin. A simpler method was devised around the middle of the 17th century when the tumbler was fashioned with a short squared shank which fitted through a hole in the lockplate. The cock was cut with a correspondingly sized hole so that it slipped over the shank on the tumbler and was then secured by a broad-headed screw. About the same time a bridle-shaped arm was fitted inside the lock to support the end of the tumbler, ensuring a better action as the bearing surface was improved and the action made a little more certain. A similar bridle was fitted on the outside of the lockplate to provide support for the frizzen screw.

21

Placing
Early Flintlocks

It may then be said that by the middle of the 17th century the French flintlock had become the universal pattern and as such was pressed into use for military and civil weapons of all types. At first its outline was essentially the same as that of the snaphaunce, with a flat, angular cock and a large lockplate. However as the 17th century progressed this plate tended to be reduced in size. Changes such as this offer some useful guidance in the dating of flintlock weapons and these features will be discussed below.

The old matchlock musket used by the armies of Parliament and King during the English Civil War was soon replaced by the more reliable and efficient flintlock and by the end of the 17th century the matchlock had been discarded as obsolete. Snaphaunce pistols were never very common in Britain or America and only in Italy did their construction continue much after the 17th century; in northern Italy, around the area of Brescia, construction of this type of weapon continued until well on into the late 18th century.

In the British economic scheme of things in the 17th and 18th centuries the colonies were regarded largely as trading outposts. It was assumed that they would import all their requirements from Britain or, at worst, would use British ships and commercial contacts even if these supplies came from territories outside British control. Thus it was inevitable that the vast majority of firearms used on the North American continent were of British origin. Some must have been of French origin for in North America sporadic fighting between French and English occurred throughout the 17th and 18th centuries and no doubt captured weapons were pressed into service particularly for the use of the local forces or militia. These local troops played an extremely active part in all the Indian and French campaigns, serving with regiments of regular British troops sent out from Europe, the regulars naturally being armed with standard British military flintlocks. Thus until the outbreak of the American War of Independence there can be little distinction drawn between English and American flintlock weapons.

In Britain the firearms industry had expanded considerably

Pistol similar to 38 but of later date since lock lacks the typical 'upswept' frizzen spring seen on earlier pistols. Made by R. Willoughby of London about 1780. Overall length 12 in. Length of barrel 6·75 in. Calibre ·6 in.

as a result of the civil wars and what had until then been a comparatively minor industry based almost entirely on London began to expand. In London the makers were mostly congregated in an area adjacent to the Tower of London for, naturally enough, it was to the regular armed forces that they looked for the greater part of their trade. With the increased demand generated by the civil wars and those of Marlborough in the late 17th and early 18th centuries there was a considerable growth in the firearms production of Birmingham, which until the 1630s had produced only a very small output. In fact it may be said with a fair degree of accuracy that Birmingham was the main source of supply, for it was here that the component parts of firearms were produced: barrels, locks and furniture—that is the fittings of pistols and long arms. In the case of military supplies the items were examined by ordnance inspectors and, if approved, were sent to London, where they were finished and made up by the London gunmakers. It would almost certainly have been in London that the export trade in firearms for America was centred. Certainly in the later part of the 18th century one firm, Ketland, became renowned for the export of its locks to North America.

What then were the flintlock weapons of the late 17th and early 18th centuries? Broadly speaking they fall into four main categories—military, personal, duelling and repeating. First there were the **military long arms**; these tended to be rugged and heavy but fairly reliable. They were fitted with a barrel normally 46 inches long and fired a lead ball approximately $\frac{3}{4}$ inch in diameter. The stock was fairly simple but possessed a pleasant shape and design. Cut into the wooden stock beneath the barrel was a trench or slot which housed the wooden ramrod for driving home the ball and powder when they had been poured down the barrel. The locks of the period were almost invariably marked with the maker's name and, to the delight of later collectors, frequently bore a date. Fittings on these early muskets were generally of iron although later brass became more common. Although heavy they no longer required the rest which had characterised the matchlock musket.

26

left Officer's fusil with bayonet, made by Hurst and marked on lockplate and barrel with number 17. Kellam Collection.

right Military blunderbuss of about 1780 complete with its wall mounting socket. The lock is marked TOWER. Kellam Collection.

Blunderbuss pistol made by Trulock of Dublin about 1800. A number of this type of weapon were produced but they were less popular than the large blunderbuss. Kellam Collection.

26, 27   Smaller than the musket was the **blunderbuss** and this form of weapon seems to have become popular quite early on in the 17th century. Its name is derived from the German *Donderbus*, literally a thunder gun, and the feature which distinguishes the blunderbuss is the belling or swamped barrel – that is one in which the internal diameter or bore expands to a greater or lesser degree towards the muzzle. It was firmly believed that this belling or opening out of the bore meant that the shot spread out as it left the barrel to increase the chances of hitting the target. This belief, largely mistaken, as experiments later showed, made them extremely popular weapons for such things as house or coach defence or use at sea with boarding parties. It seems possible that they were issued to the navy on a *pro rata* basis, decided by the number of a ship's guns, and a number are listed among the stores of artillery ferried back to England after the War of Independence. Many were fitted with brass barrels as well as brass furniture. The blunderbuss was to retain its popularity throughout the flintlock period and was replaced only when the percussion revolver made it possible to fire five or six shots from one weapon without reloading.

Military pistol made by Galton and dated 1760. The barrel is marked ROY^L DRAG^S (Royal Dragoons) and the escutcheon plate is marked T$_{22}^{5}$. Kellam Collection.

Military pistols of this period were mostly of the size known as holster pistols, fitted with fairly small-bore barrels. They fired a bullet of small diameter in comparison with the musket and its $\frac{3}{4}$ inch diameter bore. The barrels of flintlock pistols of the 17th century tend to be rather thin-walled and are frequently octagonal at the breech, changing to a circular section approximately one third of the way along the length, whilst a thickened baluster at the muzzle gave a little extra strength. During the 17th and early 18th centuries there was a tendency for the size of the bore to increase, whilst the length of barrel diminished. Most stocks were of walnut, a wood favoured throughout the entire period in Britain but replaced in America by maple.

In the early part of the 17th century the butts frequently terminated with a straight cut strengthened by a band of metal which soon developed into a flat cap. As the century progressed the square-cut end of the butt was abandoned in favour of a more rounded pommel covered with a brass or steel butt-cap. Many of the caps were decorated with carving or chiselling, often in the form of a grotesque head.

There are certain features found sufficiently often on pistols of the 17th and early 18th centuries to justify their use as identification pointers although, as with all generalisations, it must be appreciated that there are exceptions. Most pistols of this period were fitted with large lockplates and in the early flintlocks these

Pistol of about 1680 with ball butt and plain brass butt-cap. Tang screw passes upwards through stock. Gyngell Collection.

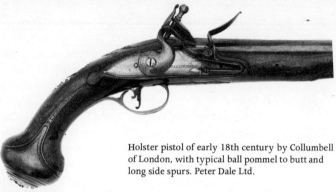

Holster pistol of early 18th century by Collumbell of London, with typical ball pommel to butt and long side spurs. Peter Dale Ltd.

bear a striking similarity to those of the wheellock and snaphaunce. Their size was sufficient to warrant the use of three screws to secure them to the stock but as the design was refined it was found that the size could be reduced and only two securing screws were required. Lockplates on pistols during the greater part of the first half of the 17th century also resembled those of the wheellock in being flat, but as the century progressed there was a gradual change to a plate with a curved surface. The angular style was also replaced by a more graceful, **banana-like shape** with a rather down-drooping line. Later the lock tended to straighten out in shape and the surface was again made flat.

Barrels also offer pointers to the dating of a pistol for the majority of those of the 17th and early 18th centuries tend to be long and with a comparatively small bore. During the early part of the 18th century the length of the barrel was reduced and, in general, the size of the bore was increased – a change usually ascribed to an improvement in the quality of the gunpowder. Barrels were secured to the stock by means of two or three lugs brazed to the underside of the barrel. Pins passed through the stock and engaged with the lugs. At the breech-end an arm, the tang, projected rearwards and this fitted into a recess cut in the stock. A screw secured the tang to the stock and on early pistols and blunderbusses this screw passed up through the stock from the trigger-guard, while on later weapons the screw passed through the barrel tang from above.

29

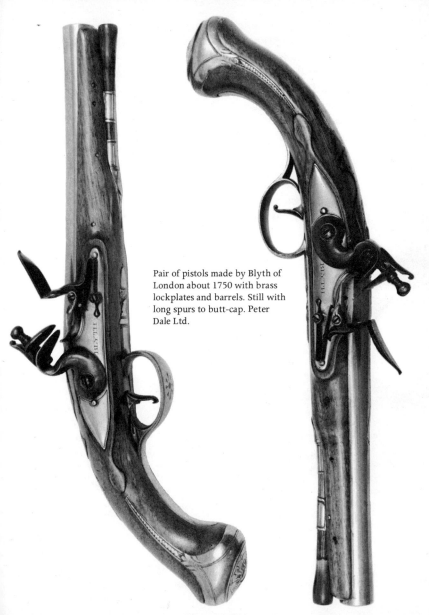

Pair of pistols made by Blyth of London about 1750 with brass lockplates and barrels. Still with long spurs to butt-cap. Peter Dale Ltd.

Stocks also exhibit certain general features such as a rather straight outline on early examples, becoming more angled at the butt in the latter part of the 17th century. From the late 18th century there was an increased use of the rather hooked type of butt. Butt-caps commonly had **long side spurs** on earlier pistols, extending well up the sides of the butt. As the 18th century progressed this feature was gradually abandoned until by the end of the century most military pistols, usually more conservative in design, had only very slight extensions to the butt-cap. Simple carving was often used by the gunmaker to **decorate the stocks** of his products although later examples of the flintlock normally lack this feature, being quite devoid of carving except for cross-hatching on the butt.

30, 31

32

Silver side-plate from Queen Anne Pistol (24), with typical military motif. Silver wire inlay also decorates the stock and there is a silver escutcheon plate.

Furniture–ramrod pipes, trigger-guards and butt plates–on early weapons was nailed on, but was later pinned or screwed into place. Late in the 18th century the barrel-pins were replaced by a wedge, a flat bar which passed through the stock and engaged with a lug near the muzzle. At the breech end the old tang system was sometimes replaced by a short hook at the breech which engaged with a metal-strengthened recess on the top of the butt.

Military firearms throughout the whole period usually carried the **monarch's cypher**–a crown and initial: I.R. or J.R. for James II; W.R. for William III; A.R. for Anne; G.R. for all the four Georges from 1714 through to 1830; W.R. for William IV and then V.R. for Victoria.

47, 57

Small pocket pistol by Perry of London with brass barrel, silver wire inlay and silver butt-cap with hallmarks for 1778. Overall length 5·5 in. Length of barrel 1·75 in. Calibre ·34 in. Giggal Collection.

Silver butt-cap from pistol (24), of unusual design for most take the form of a grotesque mask.

Cased pair of holster pistols by Durs Egg. The butts have cross-hatching and steel butt-caps, a style often used by this maker. Peter Dale Ltd.

Military flintlocks, both long arms and pistols, tended not unnaturally to be rather severe in line and stark in decoration, but in the case of civilian weapons decoration was far more prevalent and a customer wishing to impress his friends could order any style he wished. Stocks might well be carved or inlaid with any one of a great variety of precious and semi-precious materials. **Silver wire** was very popular and was worked into a great variety of patterns on the stock. A shallow trench of the desired shape was cut into the stock and a length of soft silver wire pressed into the slot. Gentle hammering made it expand slightly to grip the sides of the channel and thus stay in position. On very **good quality pieces** the trigger-guard, ramrod pipes and butt-cap might all be cast in silver, the furniture on more ordinary pieces being of brass or steel. Many flintlocks had a small shield, the escutcheon plate, set into the top of the butt and engraved with the crest of the owner.

Engraving was often used on the lockplate and trigger-guard and occasionally on **butt-cap** and ramrod pipes. Usually such engraving was fairly simple, seldom more than a series of scrolls or loops. From early in the 17th century gunmakers engraved their name or initials on the lockplate and barrels, later including their address as well, and the collector will very soon come to recognise some of the more prolific makers whose products have survived in quantity. Some makers tended to specialise in certain types of flintlock but the output of others was more varied. **Durs Egg**, of Swiss origin, produced flintlocks of very high

7, 33

11

34

35

34

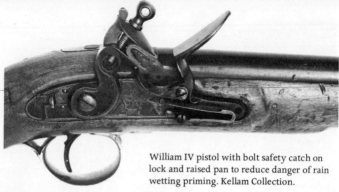

William IV pistol with bolt safety catch on lock and raised pan to reduce danger of rain wetting priming. Kellam Collection.

quality; H.W. Mortimer has acquired a reputation for his good quality blunderbusses produced at the end of the 18th century. John and Joseph Manton were renowned for the quality of their sporting guns and were patronised by the high society of the time. Such makers were able to command high prices for their products, which were often supplied in mahogany or oak cases fitted out into compartments containing the various accessories such as powder-flask, bullet-mould, oil bottle, cleaning-rod and sundry other items. Inside the lid was attached the maker's trade card, frequently engraved with a small vignette as well as the maker's name and address.

Many of the barrels and locks used by these famous London gunmakers were in fact of Birmingham origin, where they were made, tested and then sent on to London for final finishing and decoration. All barrels were proved by submitting them to the effects of a serious overload and from 1813 an official Proof House was established in Birmingham to complement that in London. After the proved barrel reached the London maker he made sure it was true and then set about polishing and finishing it. One such process was the browning of the surface by treating it with any one of a number of formulae which produced a controlled degree of rusting. When the process, a rather lengthy one, was complete, it was halted and the surface had a delightful reddish-brown layer which was not only attractive to look at but also resisted further rusting. This process emphasised the differences in texture of the component metals of the barrel and so produced a further decorative effect. Fittings such as trigger-guards were more often blued by heating them in a mixture of animal charcoal and other exotic compounds and at the correct temperature the pieces were quenched by tipping them into water. Again the attractive blue surface also served to protect, for it resisted the rusting effects of wind and water.

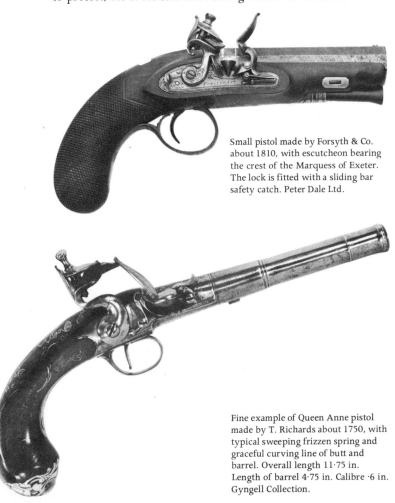

Small pistol made by Forsyth & Co. about 1810, with escutcheon bearing the crest of the Marquess of Exeter. The lock is fitted with a sliding bar safety catch. Peter Dale Ltd.

Fine example of Queen Anne pistol made by T. Richards about 1750, with typical sweeping frizzen spring and graceful curving line of butt and barrel. Overall length 11·75 in. Length of barrel 4·75 in. Calibre ·6 in. Gyngell Collection.

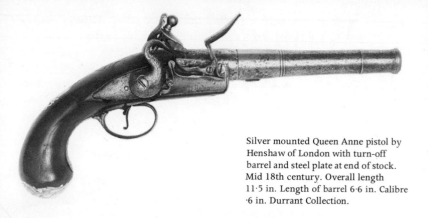

Silver mounted Queen Anne pistol by Henshaw of London with turn-off barrel and steel plate at end of stock. Mid 18th century. Overall length 11·5 in. Length of barrel 6·6 in. Calibre ·6 in. Durrant Collection.

Civilian weapons were not only more decorative but were also safer, for many were fitted with another safety device operating in addition to the normal half-cock position. The most common **36** was a **sliding metal bar** situated on the lockplate just to the rear of the cock. With the cock in the half-cock position the bolt could be pushed forward to engage with a square recess cut into the back of the cock. This device was first used in the 17th century but became more common from around 1720 and was to be found **37** in most weapons of quality by the **end of the century**. This was by no means the only system in use for there were a number of other devices designed to prevent accidental discharge.

Early in the 18th century there developed that style known to **24, 37, 38** collectors as **Queen Anne**, although such pistols were produced long after the demise of this British monarch in 1714. As a group they are generally most attractive, often with silver wire inlay and silver fittings. Although there were many variations most of the pistols are recognisable by a graceful sweeping line from muzzle to butt-cap. Some have the wood extended to just in front of the frizzen but the majority simply have a wooden butt, the rest of the pistol being all steel. Barrels are usually of the type **24, 38** which **unscrew for loading** although some pistols do have a fixed barrel and consequently a ramrod was also attached. A feature common to almost all these pistols was a very pronounced upward sweep, almost to a point, of the frizzen spring.

Variations on the Theme

One of the most serious drawbacks to any muzzle-loading firearm was the limitation of its being only a single shot weapon. One solution was to fit two barrels, one above the other, on a breech block which could be rotated. Each barrel had its own priming-pan and frizzen but a single cock was fitted to serve both barrels. Both barrels were loaded and primed and after the top one had been discharged the block was unlocked and rotated to bring the lower barrel to the top ready for firing. Less often the barrels were fitted **side by side** with two priming-pans but a single frizzen and cock. Again both barrels were loaded and primed but a close-fitting sliding plate was pushed over to cover one of the primings and the frizzen lowered. After firing the first barrel the sliding cover was pushed clear exposing the second priming; the frizzen was closed and the second barrel was then ready for firing.

From the second half of the 18th century a far more common system was that of the **tap action**. Two barrels were attached one above the other to a breech block on which was fitted a thick disc into which was cut a V-shaped recess. This disc was fitted with a grip which enabled it to be rotated through 90 degrees. Both barrels were loaded and the disc turned so that the recess was situated beneath the opening of the pan, priming powder then being placed in the recess. The block was now rotated so that the priming powder contained in the recess was moved to the internal safety of the breech block. A second pinch of priming

Pair of double-barrelled pistols
made by Hewson about 1815.
Each barrel has a separate lock
and trigger. The barrels are
browned. Peter Dale Ltd.

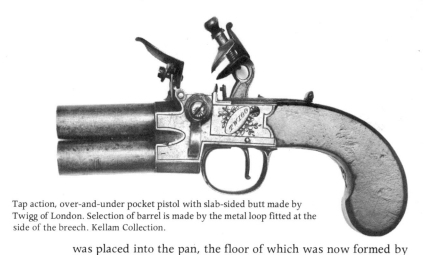

Tap action, over-and-under pocket pistol with slab-sided butt made by Twigg of London. Selection of barrel is made by the metal loop fitted at the side of the breech. Kellam Collection.

was placed into the pan, the floor of which was now formed by the edge of the rotated disc. A tiny hole connected this priming to the top barrel so that if the frizzen were then closed and the trigger pressed the barrel would fire. The disc was now turned back to expose the priming and this aligned a connecting hole through the block to the touch-hole of the lower barrel, and if the normal firing procedure was now followed the lower barrel could be fired. Tap actions were most commonly fitted to the smaller variety of pistols known as **pocket pistols**, which were very popular in Britain during the later part of the 18th century and the early part of the 19th century. Other, far more elaborate systems such as superimposed loads were tried out but weapons incorporating this system are far rarer.

41, 42

Travel in British town and country was anything but safe and it behoved the traveller to prepare for the worst. On a coach journey he probably took a blunderbuss and maybe a brace of pistols for good measure – this was certainly the armament carried on the Royal Mail coaches in the late 18th century. For the travel-ler in town whose pleasure or duty drove him out after dark heavy weapons were a hindrance and a nuisance, and a small version of the flintlock was developed. It was not a new departure for small wheellocks were common, but it was with the adoption of the flintlock that such weapons became widespread. Small versions of Queen Anne pistols were made in quantity and it was with later examples of these pistols that there developed the practice of mounting the cock not at the side of the pistol but centrally on the breech block. From 1780 onwards this type of centrally-mounted lock, the **boxlock**, was common and it was natural that it should be combined with the tap action to produce the over-and-under, tap action, boxlock pistol. With the boxlock the central mounting of the cock and frizzen meant that it was impossible for the firer to take an aimed shot, but since these weapons were only intended for use at short range this was relatively unimportant. It was obviously of great importance that these pistols should be made as safe as possible for they were to be carried around in pockets and bags, and all were fitted with

42

Tap action pistol, made by Dawes of London, with three brass barrels. Essentially the action was the same as for two barrel weapons but with three positions for the barrel selection. Peter Dale Ltd.

Boxlock pocket pistol of about 1790 marked IOHNS. Slab-sided butt with silver wire inlay. Kellam Collection.

some form of safety catch. Later versions had a concealed trigger which was fitted flush in a recess below the breech until the mechanism was set at full-cock, when it clicked down ready for firing. Even more common was the type which comprised a flat bar situated on top of the breech and fitting around the cock. If the mechanism was set to half-cock and the frizzen closed the bar could be pushed forward and not only did it engage with the cock to lock it at this safe position but also a spike at the tip slipped into a hole on the pan-cover to lock this shut. **Pocket pistols** were almost invariably fitted with turn-off barrels and consequently needed no ramrod. Butts on earlier examples are round but those of about the end of the 18th century were fitted with a **simple slab-sided butt** lacking any decoration.

43

19

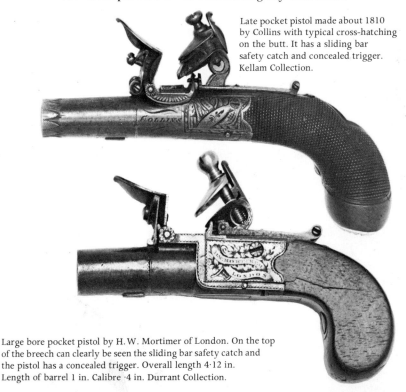

Late pocket pistol made about 1810 by Collins with typical cross-hatching on the butt. It has a sliding bar safety catch and concealed trigger. Kellam Collection.

Large bore pocket pistol by H. W. Mortimer of London. On the top of the breech can clearly be seen the sliding bar safety catch and the pistol has a concealed trigger. Overall length 4·12 in. Length of barrel 1 in. Calibre ·4 in. Durrant Collection.

Brass barrel blunderbuss pistol by W. Parker of London with spring bayonet mounted below the barrel. The blade is held in position by engaging the tip with a recess in the trigger guard. Overall length 8·5 in. Length of barrel 4·25 in. Calibre (at muzzle) ·72 in. Durrant Collection.

Another solution to this problem of the limitation of the single shot normal on a flintlock was the combining of a flintlock with another weapon—usually a sword. A small flintlock and barrel were fitted by the side of the blade just below the quillon or guard, whilst the trigger was usually fitted to the grip of the sword. Most surviving examples date from the late 18th century although the principle was much older, for swords, clubs and staff weapons had been fitted with wheellocks.

Far more common was the attached spring bayonet which was used on many pistols and blunderbusses from the latter part of the 18th century. These blades were usually triangular in section and were most often secured to the top or bottom of the barrel and less commonly at the side. If the bayonet was fastened **beneath the barrel** it was usually locked back by engaging with a specially modified trigger-guard which could be pushed backwards to release the bayonet. If the bayonet was situated **at the side** or on top of the barrel a special sliding catch was normally fitted at the breech. In an emergency the catch or trigger-guard was pushed back and the bayonet, impelled by a powerful V spring, swung forward and locked into place. It was freed by pressing a small stud and could then be folded back along

44

45

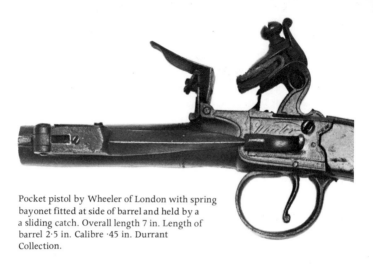

Pocket pistol by Wheeler of London with spring
bayonet fitted at side of barrel and held by a
a sliding catch. Overall length 7 in. Length of
barrel 2·5 in. Calibre ·45 in. Durrant
Collection.

the barrel and locked into position until it was needed again.

For the greater part of the 18th century there was no real distinction between the flintlocks of America and Britain. The great
majority of the colonists equipped themselves with firearms
purchased and imported from England. There was, however,
one weapon which was peculiar to the North American continent
and this was the highly accurate small-bore rifle, erroneously
called the Kentucky rifle. Its roots were European for its development seems to have occurred in those parts of the colonies oc-
cupied mainly by the descendants of Germanic settlers. In their
old countries these immigrants had been familiar with a small-
bored, heavy-barrelled and very accurate form of hunting rifle
known as the Jaeger rifle. When they went to settle in the colonies
they took with them the concept of this type of rifle and as they
became established in their new homes the few immigrant gunsmiths sought to manufacture copies of their old familiar rifle.
There were however difficulties in their way; for example walnut, a wood favoured for the stock in Europe, was difficult to
obtain in the New World. A substitute was sought and most
settled for the wood of the maple tree which was often pleasantly
patterned as well as being in many ways similar in texture to

walnut. Naturally the design of these rifles did not remain constant but by the latter part of the 18th century the **Kentucky rifle** had acquired most of its traditional features. Barrels were almost invariably heavy, octagonal, long and rifled, with a small bore. All these features—rifling, weight and length—were factors that improved the general accuracy of the rifle. Most of the rifles were fully stocked, with a characteristic gracefully down-drooping butt, slim and with a fairly deep recess to fit against the shoulder. Brass was used to embellish these weapons and into the butt was cut a recess covered with a hinged lid. This patch box had been a feature of the German hunting wheellock and Jaeger rifle and became very much a feature of the Kentucky rifles. The name Kentucky rifle appears to have originated early in the 19th century after the battle of New Orleans during the War of 1812, but the state of Kentucky, the Blue Grass State, can lay little real claim to being foremost in the field of construction of this weapon. They were certainly made in Ohio, Pennsylvania and other of the Eastern states and most students refer to them now as Pennsylvanian long rifles. However certain local features developed and these can be of great assistance in identifying the provenance of such a weapon. These long rifles played a comparatively minor, but very effective, part in the war of American Independence of 1775–1783.

Unusual over-and-under, double-barrelled pistol of about 1825 of Kentucky type. A single cock serves both frizzens, one on each barrel. Calibre ·38 in. Winchester Gun Museum.

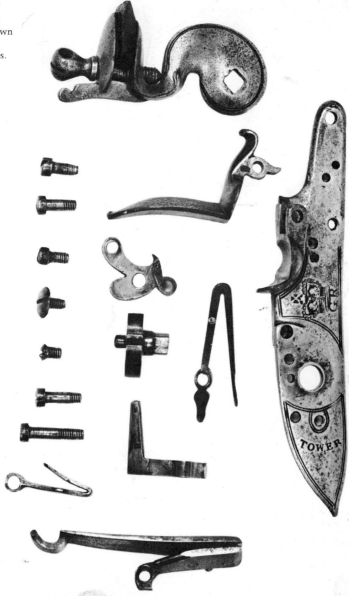

Flintlock of Brown Bess stripped down to its component parts.

With the outbreak of hostilities between the mother country of Great Britain and the North American colonies the inflow of weapons ceased. For the colonies, fighting for their very existence, the problem was crucial. Most of them of course had their own arms and many of them were equipped with standard British weapons. The militia or local force had been a very strong feature of the North American colonies and these were equipped with the British standard issue musket known as the **Brown Bess**. The Brown Bess musket saw service for well over a century although it was to develop in many forms during this long period. At the time of the American War of Independence it was of the type known as the Short Land musket and had a 42 inch barrel; it fired a ball of approximately $\frac{3}{4}$ inch diameter, was fitted with a steel ramrod, brass furniture and a standard flintlock engraved with the word Tower and a crowned G.R. Until 1764 these muskets had actually carried the date of manufacture, but owing to the reluctance of officers and troops to accept a weapon bearing a date suggesting that it was rather old, the practice was abandoned.

When the colonists found their source of supply cut off the *ad hoc* government sought to encourage the local gunsmiths to produce weapons. Local committees set up to run the government offered a number of inducements to gunsmiths to produce reliable weapons and there came into being the Committee of Safety musket which was to all intents and purposes a copy of the British Brown Bess.

It was to France that the American colonies turned for fresh supplies and these erstwhile enemies did their best to assist each other. The French were able to supply a limited number of weapons to the colonies and these were of standard **French style** and manufacture. In France the system of identifying muskets had been by year of introduction; thus a certain type of musket would be known as the 1774 model. This use of French muskets was to have a lasting effect on the design of **American flintlocks** for many of them were more or less copies of the French musket or at least resembled them very closely in detail, the same being true of their pistols. Whereas the Brown Bess musket had the

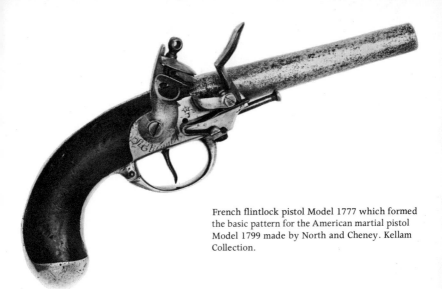

French flintlock pistol Model 1777 which formed the basic pattern for the American martial pistol Model 1799 made by North and Cheney. Kellam Collection.

barrel fixed to the stock by means of pins and lugs set beneath the barrel, the French used a much simpler method. Two or three bands could be slipped over the barrel and stock to hold them securely together and at the muzzle end a rather more complex nose cap was used. When the colonists became a little more organised and formed a central governing body this Congress decreed that in future all official weapons were to bear the words United States and, in general, this practice was followed although abbreviations were often used. However, it was obvious to the colonists that they could not rely for their firearms production on the good graces of the French and it was therefore decreed in 1794 that two National Armouries should be set up. One was at Springfield in Massachusetts, the other at Harper's Ferry in Virginia, and both were in production by 1795.

Output from both armouries was limited and insufficient to meet demands, so a system of firearms production basically the same as that used in Britain was developed. Contractors were approached and asked to supply a certain number of weapons; amongst these was an American gunmaker named **Simeon North** who acquired a position of pre-eminence in the field of firearms production. The majority of his models very closely resemble those of France in both style and general design. Those produced at Harper's Ferry bear his name and are identified by collectors by the year of contract. Simeon North produced military and duelling pistols in profusion and was active until his death in 1852.

Shortly after the return of peace in 1783 trade once again developed between Britain and the ex-colonies. Amongst the items imported were complete guns as well as parts thereof, and manufacturers such as Simeon North imported many parts from Great Britain and assembled them in the States.

American flintlock pistol of about 1775 marked Jacob Grubb, with brass barrel. Length of barrel 6·75 in. Calibre ·45 in. Winchester Gun Museum, New Haven, Connecticut.

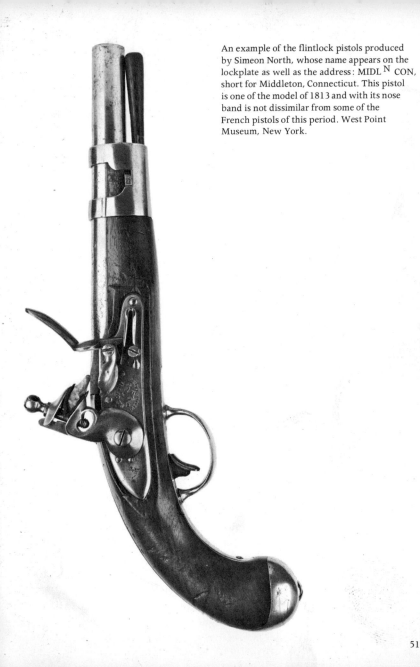

An example of the flintlock pistols produced by Simeon North, whose name appears on the lockplate as well as the address: MIDL ^{N} CON, short for Middleton, Connecticut. This pistol is one of the model of 1813 and with its nose band is not dissimilar from some of the French pistols of this period. West Point Museum, New York.

Perfection and Replacement

During the American War of Independence the British first began to experiment seriously in the field of rifled weapons. The principle of rifling with its accompanying improvement in accuracy had been known from the 16th century, but its adoption had been limited by the quite difficult technical processes involved in cutting the inside of the barrel with the appropriate number of grooves of equal depth and steady turn. There was no argument between gunmakers of the period that this undoubtedly improved accuracy, but time and cost prevented the general adoption of rifling. However, in 1776 Captain Patrick Ferguson of the British Army demonstrated in a very impressive exhibition of shooting that it was quite possible to produce not only an effective rifle but also an effective breech-loading rifle. Again the principle of **breech loading** had been known from earliest times, indeed some of the first firearms, particularly artillery, had been breech-loading. For pistols and long arms the system presented a number of problems, not least of which was the leakage of gas around the join of the means of access to the breech with a consequent loss of power. Patrick Ferguson overcame this problem quite effectively and his system incorporated a screwed plug moving upwards through the barrel, the lower end being attached to the trigger-guard. To load the Ferguson rifle the trigger-guard was given a few turns, and with its high pitched interrupted screw the plug very quickly lowered to leave a recess leading through the wall of the barrel straight into the breech. Powder and ball

53

were then poured in and a few quick turns in the reverse direction closed the plug up, and if the mechanism were now cocked and primed the rifle was ready for firing. Ferguson's rifle was efficient, simple and basically sound but for a variety of reasons, not least the death in action of its inventor, the system was never developed and after his death the small corps of riflemen that he had formed and trained was allowed to disperse.

The use of rifles in the British Army remained in abeyance until the early years of the 19th century. France and England were then locked together in a titanic struggle which raged over the whole of Europe. It was felt by some enthusiasts amongst the officers of the British army that a suitable and carefully designed rifle could have an extremely important bearing on the battles. Various tests were carried out and eventually a weapon designed by Ezekiel Baker, a gunmaker of Whitechapel, London, was selected as the best. Baker was commissioned to supply a number of them to a group of soldiers especially trained in their use, to be known as the Corps of Riflemen. The Baker rifle in some ways

Rare Hall's breech-loading flintlock action used on the U.S. Rifle Model 1819, patented in 1811 and in production until 1850. Kellam Collection.

Pair of duelling pistols with round barrels by the famous London maker, Wogdon. The ramrods differ as one has a powder measure and the other a worm for withdrawing a charge. Overall length 15 in. Length of barrel 9·62 in. Calibre ·49 in. Durrant Collection.

Duelling pistol made about 1800 by John Richards, fitted with octagonal barrel and bolt safety catch on lock. Kellam Collection.

resembled the American Kentucky, with a brass-covered patch box set into the butt and an octagonal barrel, although this had a thicker wall and was much shorter than its American relation and fired a ball of a larger diameter. The riflemen very soon proved their value although public opinion of the time tended to regard the use of such a precise weapon as the rifle as a little unsporting and tantamount almost to murder since the target was struck down deliberately and without a chance to defend himself – a strange concept.

In Britain during the latter quarter of the 18th century there was developing a special style of weapon – **the duelling pistol**. Strangely enough, Britain, the home of the duelling pistol, was not a particularly notable stronghold of duelling, this pernicious

54

practice being far more prevalent in places such as Italy, France and Ireland, but the pistol itself seems to have originated in England. They were produced in a variety of styles but most of them conformed to a general pattern. Like the Kentucky rifle accuracy was improved by giving the weapon a heavy barrel, almost invariably **octagonal** in the later versions, and by firing a comparatively small diameter bullet. The stock was very carefully designed and balanced to afford an almost automatic aim on the part of the user. The butts were sometimes of plain hockey-stick form but other pistols were produced with a saw-handled butt the spur of which settled itself comfortably in the space on the back of the hand between first finger and thumb. In order to ensure steadiness at the aim the trigger-guard on many duelling pistols had a slightly forward-curving hook-like projection and this spur offered a very firm grip to the second finger. Sights were normal on these pistols and some were of silver although some exponents of the finer points of duelling insisted that this was a bad practice since silver could catch the sunlight and distract the firer. The locks of duelling pistols were refined to give the best possible crispness of action and to this end various modifications were incorporated. To reduce friction **small bearing wheels** were fitted, either at the top end of the frizzen spring or, alternatively, on the tip of the frizzen. Inside the lock the mainspring no longer pressed directly upon the tumbler but the bearing surface was reduced considerably by the insertion of a small T-shaped link between the mainspring and the tumbler. Many of the duelling pistols were fitted with safety catches and a number have an additional internal modification known as the detent. This was an ingeniously fitted wedge-shaped section in the tumbler, so arranged that as the tumbler rotated the detent moved and, in effect, served both as half-cock and full-cock positions at the same time, making it virtually impossible for the sear to become accidentally engaged at half-cock position once the trigger had been pressed.

Decoration on duelling pistols was minimal, usually no more than perhaps some slight engraving on the lock and details of the maker's name and address deeply engraved on the lockplate

Duelling pistol by Bowls of Cork (Ireland), with plain
stock, no safety catch but small bearing wheel on
frizzen spring. Overall length 14·5 in. Length of
barrel 9·5 in. Calibre ·67 in. Durrant Collection.

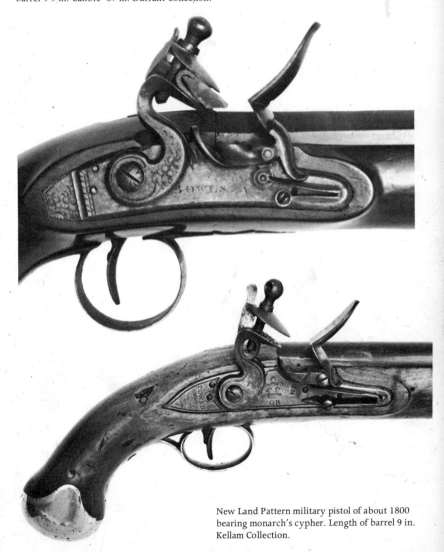

New Land Pattern military pistol of about 1800
bearing monarch's cypher. Length of barrel 9 in.
Kellam Collection.

and the top of the barrel. When the trigger was pressed there was a tendency for the weapon to be deflected slightly and the greater the pull the more likely this was to happen. Many duelling pistols were fitted with a device known as a set trigger and here an internal arrangement of levers could be adjusted so that only a very small pressure was required to withdraw the sear from the full-cock position. A small screw set in front of the trigger was used to adjust the pressure to the user's requirements.

Duelling pistols were normally supplied in pairs and these, together with sundry accessories, such as a bullet-mould for casting bullets, powder-flasks for holding gunpowder, cleaning-rods, screwdrivers and other extras were supplied in an internally divided **wood case** the compartments of which were designed to hold each particular item. Most cases were lined with green baize and inside the lid was stuck the maker's trade label.

60, 61

During the first two decades of the 19th century the flintlock mechanism had generally speaking reached the limit of development. It was reliable and consistent in performance, and with the improvements effected by the designers of duelling pistols an efficient and crisp action was ensured. Design had altered but little although there had been a tendency towards simplication and butts had become slightly more hooked-shaped, whilst the butt-cap and ball-pommel end to the butt had disappeared. It lingered on in **military pistols** but even here the spurs had almost completely disappeared from the butt-cap. One further improvement in design on pistols, introduced very late in the 18th century, was the permanently attached ramrod. An ingenious but **simple link** fitted to a lug beneath the muzzle enabled the ramrod to be withdrawn from the stock and used but kept it captive the whole time so that in an action it was virtually impossible to lose the ramrod.

57

16

Although the flintlock had become very reliable and consistent in operation it was not without its drawbacks. There was an appreciable delay between the pressing of the trigger and the actual firing of the main charge. In the case of a stationary target this delay was of little importance but for the hunter or rifleman engaged in action it could have serious effects. Most flints were

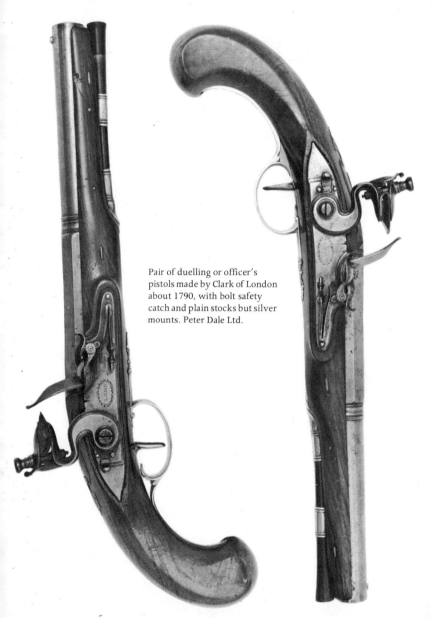

Pair of duelling or officer's pistols made by Clark of London about 1790, with bolt safety catch and plain stocks but silver mounts. Peter Dale Ltd.

Cased set of duelling
pistols by G. Moore of
London, complete
with powder-flask,
bullet-mould and
cleaning rods. Peter
Dale Ltd.

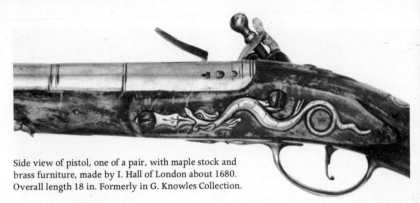

Side view of pistol, one of a pair, with maple stock and
brass furniture, made by I. Hall of London about 1680.
Overall length 18 in. Formerly in G. Knowles Collection.

reckoned to be capable of thirty shots before they required re-
placing but it was very much a matter of luck whether the sparks
were struck or not. In Scotland a country clergyman, the Rever-
end Alexander Forsyth, was applying the knowledge gained
from his hobby of chemical studies to this problem of the hang-
fire, and in 1805 he produced a very reliable system using a
fulminate compound which exploded on impact. Forsyth came
to London to develop and promote his scheme. Initially he had
little success but the idea was germinating and in a few years the
fulminate or percussion system was displacing the flintlock.
By the 1820s small copper percussion fulminate caps were firmly
established as the best system of ignition, and the flintlock was
in the process of becoming outdated and obsolete. It lingered on
for some considerable time and it was not until the 1830s that
the British Army changed over from flint to percussion. During
this transition period a few weapons were produced which incorporated both systems; thus the cautious shooter could have
a flintlock which could, by a number of comparatively quick
adjustments, be converted into a percussion lock. Manufacture
of the flintlock did not cease completely and the production of
flintlock guns for trade was to continue for many years as a
profitable side-line of the manufacturers in Birmingham. The
Red Indian, with his reluctance to accept a change, often insisted
on the flintlock although later ignition systems might well have
been available. The early trade muskets sent to the Americas had

had a certain style of side-plate fashioned in the **shape of a dragon**, and it seems from records that the Red Indian insisted upon this feature in all subsequent models. Many Indians decorated their flintlocks, one of the most popular styles being the use of a number of brass round-headed tacks hammered into the butt and stock, and later gunmakers actually made flintlocks with the tacks already hammered in.

Except for a few primitive regions the flintlock had been abandoned by the middle of the 19th century and percussion and cartridge systems were being adopted throughout the world. Some flintlocks were converted to the new system but most were simply discarded. Fortunately for collectors enormous numbers were manufactured during its century and a half of use and examples are still reasonably easily available, although prices are rising constantly as demand increases and supply diminishes.

Brass tinder pistol by Simmons complete with candle holder. These devices were used in place of the more usual flint, steel and tinder. Kellam Collection.

Acknowledgements

Photographs were kindly supplied by the author and also by the following: BMH Photographic, Crawley; Peter Dale (Insignia) Ltd, London; Paul Forrester, London; Cyril Howe Studios, Bath; West Point Museum Collections, New York; Winchester Gun Museum, New Haven, Connecticut.

COUNTRY LIFE COLLECTORS' GUIDES

Series editor Hugh Newbury
Series designer Ian Muggeridge

Published for Country Life Books by
THE HAMLYN PUBLISHING GROUP LIMITED
LONDON · NEW YORK · SYDNEY · TORONTO
Hamlyn House, Feltham, Middlesex, England

BRITISH AND AMERICAN FLINTLOCKS
ISBN 0 600 43590 3
© The Hamlyn Publishing Group Limited 1971
Printed by Toppan Printing Co. (H.K.) Limited, Hong Kong